STRESS MANAGEMENT FOR BEGINNERS

Guided Meditation Techniques to Reduce Stress, Increase Happiness, and Improve your Health, Body & Mind

Sarah Rowland

Copyright © 2016 by Sarah Rowland

All rights reserved. No part of this book may be reproduced or transmitted in any form or by any means, electronic or mechanical, including photocopying, recording or by any information storage and retrieval system without written permission of the publisher, except for the inclusion of brief quotations in a review.

TABLE OF CONTENTS

INTRODUCTION 1

Chapter 1 *What Is Stress?* 2

Chapter 2 *Process Stress In A Healthy Way – Eliminate Unnecessary Sources Of Stress* 9

Chapter 3 *Manage Stress With Food* 16

Chapter 4 *Manage Stress with Exercise* 23

Chapter 5 *Manage Stress With Sleep* 30

Chapter 6 *Manage Stress With Meditation* 37

Chapter 7 *Guided 5-Minute Meditation Session* 47

Chapter 8 *Guided 20 Minute Meditations Ession* 50

Chapter 9 *Manage Stress With Deep Breathing Exercises* 55

Chapter 10 *Maintain Activities With Positive People* 57

Chapter 11 *Daily Affirmations* 65

Chapter 12 *Positive Imagery* 71

Chapter 13 *Aromatherapy* 74

Conclusion 78

INTRODUCTION

Congratulations on downloading this book and thank you for doing so.

The following chapters will discuss causes of stress and several ways to manage and eliminate stressors in your life.

There are plenty of books on this subject on the market, thanks again for choosing this one! Every effort was made to ensure it is full of as much useful information as possible, please enjoy!

CHAPTER 1
What Is Stress ?

Stress is something we all feel on a daily basis, whether we realize it or not. It is a reaction to your daily routine and unexpected bumps in the road. It is your body's response to environmental stressors, both big and small. The body needs stress responses to react to possible threats. This is a natural, primal response that began with early humans, and has kept us safe for thousands of years.

Going way back, early humans had a very short list of threats. They worried about where their next meal came from and how to stay away from predators. The stress response prompted a reaction as a necessity for survival. They did not worry about getting to soccer practice on time and paying the bills. Unfortunately for modern humans, the stress response still exists, often causing unnecessary reactions to less life-threatening situations like problems at work or fighting with a spouse. These days, think of stress as a symptom of something that is unsatisfying in your life. Whether unhappiness with your job, financial or living situation and relationships may be prompting a response to get out of the trouble you are in.

Two types of stress exist: acute, or short term, and chronic, or long term. More and more people are suffering from chronic stress, but often have acute bouts of stress on top of their usual. As stress mounts and becomes overwhelming, panic attacks and breakdown happens. Our job is to manage stress as it comes to avoid the buildup that leads to a breakdown.

Acute stress. Have you ever noticed that when you are stuck in traffic and your anxiety is high, your focus gets sharper and you think only of the task at hand? This is your stress response kicking in, giving you the mental clarity and focus needed to deal with a lifethreatening situation. It may not be actually life threatening, but your body may think so.

Episodes of acute stress tend to string together. Think about stressors
at home, work and in your social life. While these things are

individually taxing, together, they add up to low level chronic stress. Learning to handle these individual situations in a more healthy way can decrease overall chronic stress.

Chronic stress is something we all feel every day. It is the result of the alarm clock going off, getting the kids ready for school and fighting traffic to get to work on time. Small moments of stress are needed to get your body in gear and boost energy to focus on the task at hand. Most people are under a veil of chronic stress all day long.

The body responds to stress in a number of ways. First, it releases adrenaline, frequently called the body's ‚stress hormone'. It is released by the adrenal glands to raise the heart rate, blood pressure and shortens breath to take in more oxygen for the body to use. The response goes back to our primal instincts. The body needs to

prepare to run from danger, or stand and fight, the so-called ‚fight or flight' response.

Cortisol is another stress hormone that is expressed with adrenaline. While a little cortisol once in a while is a good thing, persistent exposure to cortisol, like with several small episodes of chronic stress, has some negative effects on the body. It increases blood sugar, which can lead to diabetes over time. It decreases thyroid function, cognitive function and immune system support after prolonged bouts of stress.

The most advertised impact of cortisol is its ability to store excess belly fat. When the body thinks its survival is at stake, it will take measures to store as much energy in fat as it can. Stubborn belly fat is a common symptom of chronic stress. The adrenal glands themselves can also be affected. Adrenal fatigue happens when the glands are forced to produce excessive amounts of adrenaline, cortisol and other stress hormones as a response to stress. Over time, too little hormones are made and the body suffers from extreme fatigue, slowing metabolism and suppressed immune system.

As this continues, overall mood and attitude become affected. You become more irritable, less able to focus, and it becomes increasingly more difficult to deal with minor stresses. It will become difficult to sleep, leaving you more fatigued during the day. The less energy you have, the more susceptible you are to stress. It is a vicious circle that can only be stopped by eliminating the source of the problem, your

stress levels.

The only way to stop these negative effects is to decrease overall amounts of stress in your life. While avoiding it completely is not always possible, eliminating some sources of stress and learning to cope with unavoidable stress in a healthy way will reward you with better health overall.

Hopefully the stress of hearing about what causes stress will be the prompt you need to work on management. From here on out, we will focus on ways to deal with everyday situations in a meaningful way that reduces stress. First off, it is important to recognize possible stressors in your life. They can come from a number of places, or from one thing in particular. Common problems people face are the following:

- Family life-difficult extended family members, children and spouses can test your patience on a daily basis. While a particular person may not be the problem, making sure everyone is happy and taken care of and where they need to be can be a stressful daily task.
- Health-declining and health are a major concern. There may not be anything you can do about your own health, or that of a loved one, and that causes anxiety for the future.
- Money-worrying about paying bills and making ends meet plagues most people. Money is the key to keeping a roof over your head and food on the table.
- Work-getting along with co-workers plus increasingly demanding jobs and deadlines often push stress levels through the roof. Not to mention the stress of commuting to and from work in heavy traffic.
- Chores and household duties. If there seems to be a never ending pile of dirty laundry and dishes, you're not alone.

There will always be chores to be done, and keeping on top of them can be taxing.

CHAPTER 2
Process Stress In A Healthy Way – Eliminate Unnecessary Sources Of Stress

It is easy to turn to quick fixes to deal with stress. Crutches like smoking cigarettes and drinking alcohol seem to help calm your nerves, but only temporarily. Nicotine is an addictive drug that releases dopamine in the brain. Dopamine is a feel-good chemical that makes the stresses of life seem less severe. Smoking a cigarette is only a temporary solution, as when the dopamine wears off and the problem has not been solved, stress will begin to build up again.

Most people know that smoking is harmful to their health, yet choose to continue smoking because they are addicted, and they think it helps them deal with the problem. On the contrary, it is only good for self soothing, and when it wears off, you still have a problem to deal with.

Alcohol is very similar. It a system depressant, calming and relaxing nerves and muscles. It alters the mind so that problems don't appear as bad, and can be a temporary escape.

Unfortunately for smokers and drinkers, that temporary relaxed state is no match for the actual physical damage that they do to the body. Nicotine and alcohol are both toxic to the body. They both cause oxidative stress that begins to damage cells, and can lead to cancer over time. Alcohol also destroys the liver, the main filter keeping your blood clean.

Caffeine should be avoided during stress as well. While it is not as detrimental as smoking or drinking, caffeine is an addictive stimulant that can create hyperactivity in a person. Stress is associated with increased adrenaline, heart rate and more energy as is. Adding caffeine to the mix can increase the heart rate more, make you feel jittery and possibly lead to a panic attack. The body can only handle so much stimulation at a time, so let stress be the only factor.

Prolonged exposure to either nicotine or alcohol is detrimental to health, and could cause psychological trauma as well as physical disease. If either one of these things is your coping mechanism for stress, it is time to rethink it. Depending on how addicted you are to either substance, it may be necessary to get outside help to decrease and quit your habit. If you are a moderate user, it is possible to cut back a little at a time, and substitute healthier habits instead of alcohol or nicotine when you are stressed.

The only real way to eliminate stress is to eliminate its source. While this I not always possible, like if stress comes from a job you cannot quit, it is important to develop healthy coping mechanisms to calm you down. Start by eliminating any cause of stress that can be eliminated. Most people find they are stressed when they over extend themselves, saying yes to too many projects all at once. Know your limits, and learn to say no to people if you feel overwhelmed.

Lots of people also feel stressed by their living situations, relationships or financial circumstances. Sometimes the only way to relieve that stress is to face it head on. For example, if you have a large debt on your credit card, it is best not to ignore it. Figuring out a payment plan, even if you are paying a small amount every week, makes you feel more in control of your situation, therefore relieving stress. Sometimes not knowing the solution to your problem is more stressing than the problem itself.

There are lots of stressful situations that cannot be avoided. For example, having a sick family member is not something you cannot necessarily solve, you really just need to cope. Having healthy coping mechanisms is the key to getting through it. Here are a few examples.

Talking it out: Whether you choose to talk with a trusted friend or a professional, voicing your problems and getting it out of your head can help relieve some of the stress. It feels better knowing that someone knows what you are dealing with. It is even better if they can help come up with a solution to the problem when possible. Keeping emotions in is never a good idea, and can lead to resentment of people around you. If they do not know what your problems are, how can they help you?

Writing and journaling: If you are uncomfortable talking to others about your problems, try journaling. Getting your thoughts down on paper help you sort through them. Writing daily can help you maintain stress levels over time.

Music and Movies: using media to help you escape temporarily from your problems is a good solution. Listening to calming music or watching a funny movie can help lift your spirits and temporarily relieve stress. While it will not help solve your problem, it can keep you from overloading and having a possible panic attack. Try listening to nature sounds or classical music without words. Lyrics sometimes make things worse if a song reminds you of someone you lost or a bad time in your life. If they must have words, make sure the lyrics are happy and uplifting during times of stress.

Exercising: As we will discuss in Chapter 5, exercise can be used for stress relief. While exercise has a proven physiological benefit to reduce stress, just the act of it helps as well. Getting out for a walk, taking in some fresh air is sometimes all your mind needs to take a break and recharge. During exercise, your body takes in more oxygen, helping recharge the brain. Practicing calming techniques like yoga an Qigong help rearrange your thoughts and give more mental clarity.

Gardening, crafts and hobbies: Taking up a hobby you enjoy, especially something you can do physically, like gardening or sewing, can temporarily remove you from a stressful situation. While you can't necessarily use them to cope with acute causes of stress, like deadlines at work, doing something you enjoy when you get home will help improve your mood and outlook on your situation. Working mindlessly weeding the garden or sewing a familiar stitch allows your mind to wander, contemplating possible solutions to your problems.

Doing something productive that you like also makes you feel like you have accomplished something and if you feel stuck in a stressful situation, like waiting for someone to buy the house you are selling, can make you feel like you did something.

CHAPTER 3
Manage Stress With Food

Many people use food as a form of comfort, often overeating high fat and high sugar foods. Weight gain can certainly occur, but these types of food actually create more stress on the body. You have probably heard about allergic reactions to certain foods in the form of breaking out in hives or the throat closing up. This is the body's anaphylactic reaction to trigger foods, and there are immediate signs
that something is wrong. Some foods, however, trigger a much slower, less noticeable response that occurs in the gut. There are a few common triggers, including gluten, dairy and soy, that damage the gut lining a little at a time. Often, symptoms do not develop right away, even years after.

These triggers, and others stimulate the release of zonulin, a protein in the body that triggers gut cells to absorb nutrients. Zonulin can become over triggered if you eat the food too often. If the gut cells continue to let in goods into the bloodstream, there are

likely to be pathogenic, or just unrecognizable particles entering the blood. If the immune system does not recognize something, it attacks it. When the immune system is on high alert, the body becomes unnecessarily stressed, leading to fatigue and immune burn out. So, if you are already suffering from stress at work or in your personal life, reaching for comfort foods will likely only make your problems
worse.

As gluten, dairy and soy are the most common trigger, although there are others, reducing them in your diet can help your body remain healthy and deal with stress more efficiently. This means avoiding things like, ice cream, sugary cereal, processed snacks, and junk food in general. All of these products contain at least one, if not
all three of the common triggers, plus artificial colorings, preservatives and excess stabilizing chemicals that cause harm and stress on the body as well. Cutting them out will help increase the efficiency of your body, giving you more energy to lead an active life and manage stress.

Reach instead for foods that are naturally anti-inflammatory like fresh fruits, vegetables and meats. The simpler the food, the less likely it is to contain inflammatory substances and chemically derived preservatives. Eat a well rounded diet to make sure you are getting the proper amount and wide variety of nutrients. It's also important to balance each meal to manage your blood sugar. If out of whack, your blood sugar can spike and drop, creating a hormonal imbalance in the body.

To maintain balance, always pair a carbohydrate-rich food, like grains and fruits, with protein, like meat or nuts, or fat, like avocado
and coconut. Carbohydrates should never be eaten alone, as they spike blood sugar quickly, then drop quickly, leaving you fatigued and hungry again. Eating protein or fat along with a carbohydrate slows the increase of blood sugar because they are digested and absorbed slower.

The type of fat also matters. Pick foods that are rich in Omega 3 fatty acids like olive oil, avocado, coconut and coconut oil and fish. These fats are anti-inflammatory, unlike Omega 6 fatty acids that are inflammatory, and found in butter, canola oil and corn oil. While Omega 6 fats cannot be avoided altogether, it is best to eat more Omega 3's than Omega 6's to decrease inflammation and stress damage to your body.

Timing of meals and snacks is also very important. Make sure to eat something every 3 to 4 hours to maintain your blood sugar. Avoid having full meals that make you feel overstuffed, and go easy on your carbohydrate portions. Small, more frequent meals keep the metabolism active and running without overloading it. If you have ever overeaten, which we all do occasionally, you may have noticed feeling fatigued and groggy afterward.

Having smaller meals more often gives your body just what it needs to keep going without weighing you down. The point of consuming food in its most basic sense is to provide what your body's cells need to create energy for your daily activities. Give your body the foods it wants to create the best energy without clogging up your system with inflammatory foods that just slow you down.

Use the following sample meal ideas to get started. Consulting with a health professional about proper meals and portions for you can also help set you up for success.

Breakfast ideas:
- Two eggs cooked with olive oil (if any), sautéed peppers, mushrooms, onions and potato hash. May use any vegetables. Substitute potato with another carb, like gluten free toast if desired.
- One serving of plain, cooked oats (no sugar added). Mix with almond milk, 2-3 tablespoons of slivered almonds plus vanilla extract and cinnamon to taste. May try flax or chia seed, almond butter in place of slivered almonds.

Morning snack ideas:
- Apple plus 1-2 tablespoons peanut butter
- 4-5 gluten and soy free crackers with 2 slices lunch meat

- ½ cup fruit of choice with 1-2 tablespoons nuts

- Lunch ideas:
- Garden salad with grilled chicken, olive oil drizzle and vinegar for dressing. May substitute tuna or lunchmeat in
- place of grilled chicken.
- Lettuce wraps with lunchmeat and cut vegetables. Use olive
- oil or avocado slices for dressing.
- Afternoon snack ideas:
- Fruit and nut bar (Larabar is gluten, dairy and soy free)
- 4-5 gluten and soy free crackers with 1-2 tablespoons peanut or almond butter.
- ¼ cup hummus plus carrot sticks

Dinner ideas:

- Baked or grilled salmon with asparagus and baked potato. Use olive or coconut oil to sautee asparagus.
- Pasta night- Marinara sauce with ground beef or turkey over small helping of gluten free pasta. Use spaghetti squash or zucchini noodles as a substitute for paste. Serve with a side

- salad.
- Steak with broccoli and rice.

Dessert ideas:
- Fruit with natural cocoa spread (should be soy and dairy free)
- Dark chocolate square with small serving of fruit
- Dried cranberry or raisin with nuts

Getting your diet under control will help maintain or lose weight, stabilize your blood sugar and lower inflammation in your body. It is important to feed your body properly so that it may function at optimal levels. It will repay you by giving more energy, more mental clarity and function, and will be less affected by outside stress.

CHAPTER 4
Manage Stress with Exercise

The benefits to exercise are seemingly endless. Being active lowers blood pressure, cholesterol, blood sugar levels as well as keeping muscles strong, including your heart.

When it comes to stress, exercise helps for a number of reasons. First is the anecdotal benefit of getting your problems off your mind, or at least giving you the chance to think them through. Going for a long, leisurely walk gives your mind time to wander, and often gives the walker a little bit of clarity in dealing with whatever stressful situation they happen to be dealing with. This works especially well for people that are constantly moving from one thing to another, like in fast-paced work environments. The mind has no distractions
except the sound of footsteps, forcing it to slow, process and rest.

More involved exercise, like an aerobics class or yoga seems to give the brain rest as well. All mental focus has to be trained on the task

at hand to do all the moves in aerobics or yoga. The mind concentrates on body position and coordination, rather than deadlines and bottom
lines.

Exercise is important on a cellular level as well. During exercise, the hormone norepinephrine is released, which moderates body's stress response. It is a stress hormone, just like adrenaline and cortisol, yet its function is really to create awareness and mental clarity in the mind, so that it may react quickly and appropriately to a stressful
situation.

Exercise also releases endorphins, or happy hormones that increase feelings of satisfaction and happiness, the exact opposite feelings stress is associated with. They help reduce the body's perception of pain and often act like a sedative. While these effects can also be seen from a cocktail of prescription medication, exercise is the natural way to boost your feel-good hormones.

Stressful situations naturally cause the release of adrenaline, the hormone that preps body muscles to run away from a threat. This is a primal response that doesn't always work well in modern times. Most likely, you will not be running away from your desk and your boss or your family commitments. Or should you? That adrenaline will sit idle in your muscles until it is used, making you feel tense and edgy. A bit of exercise uses up that adrenaline, making you feel more calm.

Just about any exercise will do, as long as it is done consistently throughout the week and you don't over do it. As with any new exercise routine, it is important to know your limits and build your stamina over time, rather than doing too much and adding more unnecessary stress on your body. Here are a few types of exercise to try adding to your daily routine.

Cardio-walking, jogging or running will give you the immediate adrenaline release you need to calm down and refocus your attention on the task at hand. Making sure to do this daily, or every other day helps maintain stress levels. Using it as a coping mechanism during particularly stressful times is also much better than turning to food, cigarettes or alcohol.

If you are not used to running or walking, take it slow. Any bit of exercise will make improvements in your stress level, so even a quick 5-minute walk around your office building with help reduce your worries. As you build stamina, increase the time or the intensity of exercise for added benefits.

Yoga- known for its mind/body benefits, yoga is a great, low impact exercise to start incorporating. There are several forms of yoga, but all are centered around specific body poses that are held to stretch and increase muscle strength to relieve stress. Poses vary from standing, sitting and laying down. You will be taught to breathe a little differently while holding poses, allowing for a better stretch and strengthening of muscles. The practice of deep breathing in itself is calming, which will be discussed more in Chapter 10. It is meant to be calming and relaxing, and is not a test of flexibility. The idea of 'practicing' yoga is to improve upon your own strength and flexibility, not to compete with others.

If you are not familiar with yoga, taking an introductory class is the best place to start. Online tutorials are okay, but it takes too much focus to pay attention to your computer screen. Taking a class allows you to simply listen to instructions and take an occasional glance at your instructor to make sure you're doing it right.

Try a beginners class first. Advanced classes and hot yoga classes are meant for those who already have a good idea of what to do. While not hard, it adds another level of focus and capability you may not have as a beginner. Taking an introductory class gives you time to learn some standard poses and get into the swing of things. You will
likely feel much less stress after your first class, but if you don't, try it again.

The stress of trying something new could hinder your first try. Also, make sure you find a teacher that you are comfortable with, as technique can vary, and you may find that some teachers explain less and move quicker through poses.

After you learn some things, you will likely have a few poses that you like best, and these could always become your go-to poses to do at home, or when you are feeling particularly stressed.

Tai Chi- this ancient Chinese practice is like yoga, but with more fluid movement. It is sometimes referred to as ‚meditation in motion'. While its exact origins are unknown, it is said it was developed to be a branch of martial arts. Regular practice promotes overall wellness through better flexibility, balance, increased feelings of inner peace and less depression. Since it involves fluid motion, it does add a level of cardio workout, although light, and is low impact
for joints.
Medical studies link practice of Tai Chi to decreased symptoms of Parkinsons, diabetes and fibromyalgia, and decreases the risk of chronic heart failure and depression.

Motions are meant to be done fluidly, meaningfully and without break. There are several offshoot techniques, each a little different, but rooted in the same concept. Just like yoga, a beginners class to learn the basics is a great place to start.

Qigong- another Chinese-derived exercise is a combination of yoga and Tai Chi. It combines the breathing exercises of yoga with the fluid motion of Tai Chi. There are several types, including a hardcore martial arts version, but the most commonly known practice is for stress relief, joint pain reduction and balance. Like Tai Chi, consistent practice shows considerable improvement in conditions like arthritis, pain, cancer and overall stress. Followers attest to having more energy and more tolerance to stress.

Whatever type of exercise you choose, make sure to start small and not over tax your body. Pick something that fits relatively well with your daily routine so that the stress of adding another thing to your to do list doesn't bring you down. The exercise must be enjoyable. We are trying to increase levels of happiness, not bring you down.

CHAPTER 5
Manage Stress With Sleep

Sleep, as a definition, is a mental state where your body is relaxed and still, and your mind, body and soul are given time to recharge. You should be getting 7-10 hours of restful sleep per night to be fully charged in the morning. There are several factors that can cut this time short, stress being a major factor.

As you sleep, your brain goes through several cycles of REM sleep, deep sleep cycles that recharge the brain with oxygen, allowing cells to recover. Interestingly enough, a REM cycle is associated with vivid
dreams, eye movement under the lids, which would seem like a restless sleep. The REM cycle occurs toward waking hours which is why it is important to get uninterrupted sleep to facilitate this process.

If you are stressed, you are probably either get too little sleep, have a hard time falling asleep and wake up groggy and tired. Like we said before, chronic stress causes the release of adrenaline, and unless you do something about it, will make you feel edgy and tense. This only goes away by using the adrenaline that has already been produced, and stopping the addition of more by getting your stressors under control. Easier said than done, but lots of little changes to your bedtime routine can help you sleep better.

Reducing stressors before bed: The only real way to cut off stress is to stop thinking about the thing that is bothering you. Avoid going to bed feeling tense and awake. Your muscles should be relaxed and your mind turned off. That may seem unreasonable, as you have undoubtedly tried, but try these few things to alleviate your stress.

- Cut off all electronic use at least an hour before bedtime, no cell phones or computers specifically. The glow of artificial light from phones and TVs keeps you up, and if you choose to look at work items, will keep you up longer. Unplug.
- Read a leisure book or magazine. Pick up a paper copy of something you have wanted to read. Pick a book that is

unrelated to your daily tasks, like a fiction novel, that can take your mind to a completely different place.
- Practice yoga poses before bed. Take a few minutes to do some of your favorite poses to focus your breathing and release some stress from your muscles.
- Write to relax. Sometimes getting your thoughts down on paper helps clarify your thoughts. Whether it is writing through an emotional situation or simply making a list of things you don't want to forget tomorrow at work, doing something physical and tangible seems to give the brain some relief.
- Try deep breathing to calm yourself. The practice of deep breathing helps focus the mind on just breathing, rather than other things. As your mind eases, you will be able to drift off.

Specific exercises will be discussed in Chapter 10.

While these techniques might not work for everyone, or in every situation, they are a good start. Consider the possibility that you have a functional issue with rest. You may have trouble sleeping because you had caffeine too late in the day, or because your body's natural circadian rhythm is disrupted. Your body is designed to release melatonin and taurine at specific times to put you to sleep.

Should that rhythm be off, it will be difficult to sleep until this balance is corrected. Melatonin and taurine supplements are available to try. In general, melatonin helps you fall asleep and taurine helps you stay asleep. Try one based on which problem you are having. Always check with your doctor to determine if supplementation is safe for you.

Medications are also available over the counter and by prescription to help you sleep immediately however, they have many negative side effects including waking groggy and sleep walking. Doesn't sound like you will be getting much beneficial rest with these, and they can be habit forming. It's best to stick to natural solutions whenever possible.

Another possibility is that you have sleep apnea. Most sufferers do not realize they have it, but it greatly effects quality of sleep. Sleep apnea is a condition where breathing is halted and oxygen is decreased to the brain. The decrease in oxygen causes the person to feel groggy and tired upon waking, as their brain has not fully recharged.

The affected sometimes appear to stop breathing, then suddenly take a gasping deep breath, all while asleep. This problem is common, but not limited to, people who are overweight or obese. Excess weight can cause pressure on the lungs and trachea, making it harder to breathe. Structural abnormalities could also cause it.

Snoring is another common symptom. This condition is dangerous, and should be treated properly. If a family member has complained that you snore, don't just brush it off. It could be a symptom of sleep apnea. Mention it to you doctor so that they may do appropriate testing to diagnose. Use of a CPAP machine pumps extra oxygen into the lungs through a breathing mask worn at night.

Your sleeping environment plays a big role in restful sleep as well. A deep, restful sleep without interruptions can be difficult to get. Light and noise pollution as well as restless pets and children can keep you
from getting a full 8 hours of sleep. While these things are unavoidable, they do lead to increased stress during the day.

You can at least work on the things you can control. For example, the temperature in the room is important because you could either be too cold or too hot, prompting addition and subtraction of blankets all night long. Most people prefer a cooler room, so that they may have a blanket on and not be too hot.

Light and sound can be controlled to a point as well. Addition of white noise, either from a specifically programmed sound machine, or something as simple as a ceiling or stand alone fan can create a hum that blocks out all other external sounds. Use heavy shades or sleeping masks to block out all light. The idea is to turn off the senses of sight and sound that keep the brain active longer than necessary. Using aromatherapy scents like lavender also have a calming effect on the mind, which may lull you to sleep faster. More on that in

Chapter 12.

CHAPTER 6
Manage Stress With Meditation

Meditation is a powerful tool for stress relief and management. Meditation, in its simplest terms, is practicing to become more mindful. While there are several offshoots, which will be discussed, the general idea is to sit still and maintain your focus on one single thought. Whether that be a sound, your breath, or a mantra, the idea is to focus your attention and stop thinking about the stressors in your life.

Meditation originated in Hindu culture over 5,000 years ago, although most researchers believe it started long before this, but written word does not go back that far. Carved figures were found by archaeologists working in the Indus Valley in the early 1900's showing meditation poses and Sanskrit words for chanting. Hinduism was the first major religion to practice meditation. Buddhism was later developed, centered around the meditation practice for spiritual enlightenment.

Similar practices developed in other regions around the world, including North America. Native Americans used meditation techniques involving high heat to create a heightened sense of awareness in sweat lodges. They would also dance to drums, entering a trance-like state. A similar practice in Istanbul, the Sufi Whirling Dervish dance, where people listen to music, internally recite prayer and spin in circles is meant to let go of inhibitions and connect a person to their inner self. The rituals and movements also have several other religious aspects, a testament to the God, Allah.

The Aborigines in Australia used sound techniques from didgeridoos, and Islamic and Christian prayer was, and still is a form of meditation. The need for spiritual enlightenment and centering is something all humans share. While we may each do it in a different way, we are all connected by the search for spiritual enlightenment.

Two main types of practice exist, upward meditation and downward meditation. The idea of upward meditation is that energy is drawn up and out of the body through meditation creating a so-called out of body experience. The mind becomes detached from the body. Downward meditation does the opposite, bringing energy into the body, giving a higher sense of connection between the mind and body.

There are many ways to use meditation for specific purposes. For the beginner, the purpose is usually to relieve stress and focus on positivity. More specific practices get the meditator to get in touch with their emotions, or focus on the realities of life, or the opposite, provide an escape with fantastic methods. Meditation can be used as therapy for a number of conditions, prompting the meditator to get in touch with thoughts and emotions, and work through them in their own mind. This is part of the process to enlightenment.

Meditation has so many benefits in stress management and in other aspects of life. People who practice report having a greater sense of inner peace. This often stems from lower blood pressure, decreased tensing of muscles, decreased restlessness and better sleep. All of these things reduce the total stress on the body, allowing it to function properly and handle stress as it comes in a more effective way. A study done by Harvard in the 1970s created and tested methods of meditation and found tangible ways to measure these successes of meditation. Their participants were less anxious, able to accomplish more during the day and had lower risk for medical ailments like heart disease and depression.

A word of caution when exploring your meditation options. Meditation is an individual process. It only requires your mind, body and focus. Be weary of practitioners who tell you that other things, like special mats or candles or tapes and videos are required. They may just be looking to sell you something that will not necessarily enhance your meditation process.

Other practitioners may want to try and convert you to a new religion or spiritual practice. While exploring these options is a necessary step to enlightenment, if you feel uncomfortable in any way, or feel that a practitioner is motivated by anything other than your well being, you have the right to cease the relationship. Research and read reviews if you decide paying for a class is the right option for you. Find out before investing if the service you are signing up for is worth the money.

Heart Rhythm Meditation: this method is downward centered, creating more awareness and energy inside the body. Listening to your heartbeat, rather than your breath is better for some people, because sometimes your breath becomes controlled, and quickens the more you focus on it. People report quickening breath leading to panic attacks when they focus on it too much. The heartbeat is less changed by focusing on it, making it a better pulse point for attention.

Simply sit in an upright position, close your eyes and place the fingers from one hand on the wrist of the other. Press gently and feel your pulse, and let this sensation be your guide to focus your attention. As you feel the heartbeat, internally hear the words ‚Sat Nam' for the contraction and relaxation of your heart.

Mantra meditation: The idea of mantra meditation is to focus your thoughts on one singular word or sound. The sound is externalized and chanted. You commonly hear the chant ‚Aum' or ‚Ohm'. The chant is meant to be a primal sound that, when chanted, resonates through the entire body. It can be felt as a vibration in the body that creates a sense of calm, relaxation, and focus only on this sound. As you say it, do not try to reach a certain octave or note, simply let it flow from your lungs. The note should feel natural and deep coming from your throat. There really is no right way to do this, as long as it feels calming and relaxing to you. This practice can be done as part of a guided class, but the chanting of others around you can become distracting. However, others feel that chanting as a community offers different sensations that can be beneficial as well.

Transcendental Meditation: This is an offshoot of mantra meditation, in which a specific process was created by one practitioner. Maharishi Mahesh Yogi. To quote him,

‚THE GOAL OF TRANSCENDENTAL MEDITATION IS THE STATE OF ENLIGHTENMENT. THIS MEANS WE EXPERIENCE THAT INNER CALMNESS, THAT QUIET STATE OF LEAST

EXCITATION, EVEN WHEN WE ARE DYNAMICALLY BUSY'. STRESS MUST BE RELIEVED IN ORDER TO ACHIEVE SPIRITUAL ENLIGHTENMENT, AND THAT IS DONE THROUGH
MEDITATION.

As the most recognizable type of meditation, this involves sitting still in the lotus position and chanting an internal mantra. Usually, you will focus on one specific word that has a neutral meaning, something that doesn't evoke any particular emotion. The word itself does not matter.

The word should be said internally, repeated at a pace that keeps your focused on the word, with no mind wandering. For example, should you say ‚faithful' as your word, give it a few seconds before you say it again. Keep this pace for a minute, and if your mind begins to wander at this pace, say it with less space between. This will help keep your focus on the single word, rather than slipping back into thoughts of the day.

There are many classes available that teach the process of Transcendental Meditation, but the description above is pretty much it. This can be done anywhere, like in a quiet room at home, or in your office chair at work. The environment and the position in which you do this are less important than maintaining the overall focus. Classes may be helpful for some if they do not have an environment to meditate in that is quiet and free from external distractions. Sometimes getting out of the physical area where stress occurs helps the process significantly.

Several sources say that practicing this technique for about 15 minutes 2-3 times per day for the best results. When practiced regularly, followers experience less stress overall, more mental clarity and a greater awareness of the world around them.

Passive meditation: This method is probably one of the easiest to begin with. A sound, like a gong or bell can be used to create a steady repeating sound. The meditator simply has to focus on this external sound, rejecting all other thoughts. The only downfall for this type of guided meditation is that it may not work for each individual in every situation. Unlike transcendental meditation, the meditator relies on an outside source for their focus sound, rather than creating it from within. It does not allow for change in the sound, or change in frequency. Depending on your mental state, your mind may wander if it cannot fully engage in the sound provided.

The nice thing is, you can use pre-recorded sounds at home to create a more calming environment. Should the sound not work for you on a particular day, change or add your own internal mantra to help focus your mind.

Mindfulness: this technique is different from the rest, and rejects the idea that you must focus on one thing to escape from stress in your life. In this method, sitting still and letting any and all thoughts enter your head allows you to time to think, but not act. This method is incredible useful in work environments. You can sit for 5 or 10 minutes simply thinking about the task at hand before saying or doing anything. Sometimes this is the mental clarity you need to continue on with confidence.

You are invited to try all types of meditation in order to find what works best for you. Many people try one type, decide it is not for them, and simply give up. Try several things, like you would with exercise classes before you make that decision. Finding a method, whether it be one of these or a combination of methods is highly individual, and can also develop and change for each person over time. There are no rights and wrongs to meditation. Trying to fit a particular mold may actually create more stress, so just do what is comfortable for you.

CHAPTER 7
Guided 5-Minute Meditation Session

Try this 5-minute guided meditation to calm yourself during stressful situation. This short practice will help you gather your thoughts and calm your breathing. This can be done as a guided meditation, by listening to this audio book, or these techniques can easily be translated into a self-guided process to use at your desk at work, in the car or at home. Let's begin.

Start by getting in a comfortable position. Sit so your back, hips and legs are comfortable and not strained. You may sit cross-legged, legs straight or in a chair. Center your spine over your hips, straight up, head straight and in line with your spine. Imagine a string is holding your head and spine, pulling it upward toward the sky. Close your eyes.

Take a deep breath in, hold it for a moment, then release slowly, feeling the pressure and anxiety being released with your breath. Continue breathing normally, in and out.

Feel your breath slow as you begin to relax.

Focus on your finger tips. Feel the energy pulse through them as you remain still.

Focus on your toes. Feel the energy pulse through them as you remain still. Slowly move your hands to your stomach. Gently place your palms on your belly.

Feel your belly expand as you steadily breathe in and out.

Feel the energy flowing between your palms and belly.

Sit like this in silence for a few moments. Let any thought that enters your mind to linger there. Do not force them out or try to change them, just listen to your inner thoughts.

When you're ready, slowly open your eyes.

Remain still for a moment as you re-enter your world.

Begin again refreshed and awake.

Repeat this mini-session any time you are feeling fatigued or overwhelmed. Pair it with longer meditation sessions for a better sense of inner peace every day.

CHAPTER 8

Guided 20 Minute Meditations Ession

Try this guided meditation session daily, multiple times daily if needed. Practice first thing in the morning before you start your day to get a renewed sense of focus and purpose for the day. This may also be done at night to calm your nerves and prepare you for sleep. Find a quiet space in your home free of external distractions like light and sound. The room should be dimly lit, allowing for your eyes to relax. It should also be free of irregular sounds. If necessary, try running a fan or other white noise to create a steady sound that is less jarring. The room should be a comfortable temperature, you should not be hot or cold. It is only distracting. Ask others around you to give you the quiet time you need, so that your session is not interrupted. Let us begin.

Start by getting in a comfortable position. Sit so your back, hips and legs are comfortable and not strained. You may sit cross-legged, legs straight or in a chair. Center your spine over your hips, straight up, head straight and in line with your spine. Imagine a string is holding your head and spine, pulling it upward toward the sky. Close your eyes.

Take a deep breath in, hold it for a moment, then release slowly, feeling the pressure and anxiety being released with your breath. Sit still for a moment, taking note of the slowing of your breath as you relax. Now I want you to focus your attention on a single word. "peaceful". This word will symbolize your state of mind, the state of your body and your only intention from this moment forward. It is everything. Say the word to yourself in your mind.

What feelings does this word bring forward?
Peaceful (wait 3 seconds), peaceful (wait 3 seconds), peaceful (wait 3 seconds, repeat for 2-3 minutes. Stay silent for another minute) Slowly take a deep breath in, hold it for a moment, then release slowly, feeling the pressure and anxiety being released with your breath.

Take a moment to feel the energy pulsing through your body. Focus on the top of your head. Feel the energy move down your spine. Feel the pulsing energy as it rushes toward your fingertips. Feel it course through your legs, extending all the way down to your toes. Feel it come back up as it circles through your heart, your organs, bringing fresh life.

Slowly take a deep breath in, hold it for a moment, then release slowly, feeling the pressure and anxiety being released with your breath.

Let your mind relax, focusing only on the sound of my voice. Know that at this moment, you are perfectly calm. You are solely in control of your body, your mind and your surroundings. Nothing can touch the power inside of you. You can move the Earth. You create the breeze that is blowing through the trees. You are the energy that moves rivers of water. The tide that makes waves slowly breaking on the beach. You are the creator of all energy. Everything is under your control.

Slowly take a deep breath in, hold it for a moment, then release slowly, feeling the pressure and anxiety being released with your breath.

Sit in silence and allow in any thought that comes to mind. Do not try to suppress any thought, let it linger, grow and change.
(moment of silence for 4-5 minutes) Slowly take a deep breath in, hold it for a moment, then release slowly, feeling the pressure and anxiety being released with your breath.

In a few moments we will say, "Aum". Take a deep breath and create sound as you exhale. Let the sound flow through you, taking its natural course. Let it sound how it wants to sound.
Now take a deep breath and say "Aum". Let the sound continue until you run out of breath.

Again, breathe in and exhale "Aum".

Slowly take a deep breath in, hold it for a moment, then release slowly, feeling the pressure and anxiety being released with your breath.

Slowly open your eyes but focus only on the sound of my voice.
You will now begin again. You are relaxed, calm and confident. Wherever you go from here, you are in control. You are in charge of your own destiny.

Your problems are but small pebbles on a sandy beach. They can simply be washed away with the waves you have created.
Go forth renewed, relaxed and clear.

CHAPTER 9
Manage Stress With Deep Breathing Exercises

Deep breathing is really the center of all relaxation practices. From yoga to meditation and aroma therapy, focus on the inhale and exhale of breath is used to control anxiety levels and create a sense of calm in the body.

The nice thing about deep breathing exercises is the ability to do it just about anywhere. Certain methods require you to be in certain positions, but they can be modified to be done spur of the moment at your office or in the car if necessary.

Simply focus on your breath, in and out. Sit with your back in good posture, or lay flat on your back. Place one hand on your chest and one on your stomach. Take a few breaths normally and pay attention where your breath comes from, either the belly or the chest. It comes from the chest in most people. As you become conscious of this, focus on taking deep breaths that fill your belly. Use your abdominal muscles to pull as much air in as possible, then release slowly, allowing your muscles to push out every last bit of air.

As more oxygen enters your system, your brain will recharge, your heart rate will slow, and you will become more relaxed. Repeat each session for about five minutes any time you are feeling stressed for a breath of fresh air. This can be done in the office, at home or in the car (while it's in park!).

CHAPTER 10

Maintain Activities With Positive People

Many people tend to shy away from their usual activities when they are stressed, anxious or depressed. They feel they cannot handle any more stimulation, and often choose to be solitary. The tendency to withdraw from social situations is actually detrimental to the situation, especially with depression. Sometimes it can be difficult to pick yourself up and force yourself to get out to a party, or even have lunch with a friend, but the healthy benefits it provides once you get there are usually immediate.

Besides stress relief, socializing has been shown to boost the immune system, fighting off the cold and flu, and may actually help you live longer. Socializing, especially in older adults keeps the brain engaged and decreases your risk of developing dementia. When it comes to stress, engaging in social activities boosts the mood and helps distract you from your problems, if only for a short time. Take time to reconnect with people, get your mind of things that are stressing you. It is so easy to get caught up in your own thoughts. The more you dwell on your negative thoughts, the bigger they become.

There is one caviot, however. The people you associate with should be positive thinking, supportive people. Hanging around with people who only want to complain about their problems, complain about other people, and have nothing to offer but negativity will not reduce your stress levels. Sometimes that means going outside your normal circle of friends to find some relief. Here are a few ideas to get out there:

Take an exercise class: Bonding with a new friend in your exercise class is a great way to break the ice. You are both there to do a positive thing, improve your health. Make it a point to say ‚Hello' and introduce yourself to someone in the class. They may be looking for a new friend as well. Even if you don't talk to someone new, taking a class can still give you a sense of community you would not get from doing an exercise video alone at home, or taking a walk by yourself. Everyone in the class is there to do the same thing, and are there voluntarily. By default, you all have something in common, and that can help build new friendships.

If your social skills are more advanced, consider joining a sports team if you have the time. Playing team sports like volleyball or softball keep you engaged and constantly interacting with your teammates. You will celebrate wins together, practice together and build new relationships.

Volunteer: Whether it be at your local soup kitchen or helping organize an event, volunteering will make you feel good because you are helping other people. You will likely also be sharing your time with like-minded positive people who want to help as well.

Getting active in your community will put you face to face with someone you have yet to meet. Building friendships in the community will give you a place to turn when you are having a difficult time. You may also learn some new skills, boosting your self-confidence and mood. Everything about it says stress relief.

If you're not sure where to get started, keep an eye out on community bulletin boards and the local newspaper for advertisements of upcoming events and volunteer requests. It may be helping organize the town parade, rebuilding something, or gathering donations for a family in need. Find a cause that speaks to you so the take does not feel like work. Remember that the key to stress relief is doing something enjoyable to boost endorphins, it should not stress you out even more.

We said before that over extending yourself is often a cause of stress. Make sure the volunteer activity you decide to do fits in your schedule, and does not take more commitment than you can offer. A one-time volunteer opportunity is a good place to start. Something like raking leaves on the town green will likely take only a few hours with no other commitment. This will give you a chance to get out and do something without a long term commitment.

Networking events: Most people think of networking events as a way to get in touch with colleagues or make new customers for their business. This may not seem like a good way to relieve stress if your main issue is work. While most events like this are set up with workrelated themes, it I possible to network with people in other ways. First off, socializing with your co-workers or people in the same field as you has its benefits. If you do attend one of these events, talk only a little about your business, but spend a good deal of time trying to get to know people on a personal level. Most likely, those you speak with don't want to focus on work after hours either. Also, taking the time to know someone could inadvertently get you some new clients, as you become an approachable, relatable human being.

If your main source of stress is social anxiety, networking and carrying on a conversation with a stranger may make your blood pressure rise. While the point is to relieve stress, remember that sometimes facing your problem head on is the only way to fix it and decrease stress. For lots of people, conversation is not a natural thing. It takes mental preparation and great focus to carry it out. Think of networking as a job skill (because it really is). You did not learn how to use the computer system at work overnight, but you eventually did. The more you practice communicating with people, the better you will become, and the less stressful it will be.

If work events don't seem appetizing, think about your favorite hobby. For instance, let's say you really like knitting or crafts. Seek out a craft fair or local knitting group. Meeting people with similar interests is a great way to get the conversation started, boosting those endorphins. Picking up some new skills from new people will help increase your self confidence as well. You may even make some new friends.

Play with your pet: If interacting with humans has no appeal to you, especially if part of your stress is social anxiety, starting with a pet may be a good transition. Interacting with a dog or cat is much less taxing than carrying on a conversation with a person. Pets just like to play, get pet and snuggle. While they sometimes act up, they don't talk back, and they relieve stress.

If you have a pet already, spend some more time with them. Take your dog out for a long walk, play ball in the yard, or simply take more time to acknowledge and appreciate that they are there. Remember that your dog is always excited to see you when you get home, regardless of whether you blew a big meeting at work or not. They don't care about anything except you. Think of this often at work to lift your spirits. Think about how they jump around, wag their tails and lick you to say hello as you walk in the door. It will give you something to look forward to. Cats are great too, but their love is a bit less enthusiastic. They may just brush up against your leg or curl up next to you on the couch, but the love is the same. Many studies have shown that pet owners have less anxiety, lower blood pressure and decreased risk of depression.

Taking your dog to the dog park or out on a walk also attracts other dog loving people. Just as it is important for your dog to socialize with other dogs, you should be socializing with their owners. Simple conversations lead to play dates, a few laughs and a new friend.

If you don't have a pet, you may think about getting one, but remember that having an animal takes a commitment of time and resources. You should not get a pet if you don't have proper time to spend with it, the animal will suffer. Instead, volunteer at a local animal shelter. There, you can play with and walk dogs, or sit and snuggle with cats and kittens. While you are not committing to them long term, you can make their day, and yours by spending a little time with them.

CHAPTER 11
Daily Affirmations

Your day should revolve around positivity, and the source of that positivity must begin with you. What was the last thing you thought about yourself? Did you praise yourself for a job well done, or did you internally scold yourself for not doing something right? Would you speak to your loved one the same way if they had done something wrong? Likely not, so why would you speak to yourself that way.

It is so easy to get down on yourself for something you screwed up, or just about how you feel about yourself in general. One small negative thought can snowball in your head to become a blizzard of negativity, nit-picking every little thing about yourself. Your thought could start out as, ‚I really don't like how my body looks in this shirt.' In essence, it is really the shirt that is the problem, not your body, but what it turns in to is, ‚I don't look good in anything, I hate my body, how could anybody love me?'

While this may seem a little wild, the mind's natural process is to dwell on the little things until they become big things. It is important to remind yourself of this before your thoughts get out of control.

The mind is a very interesting thing. Your brain's nerve and thought system creates habits. It creates pathways of neurons that become familiar in order to save time and streamline the processing of thought. If your thoughts are always negative, that nerve pathway will become a highway that all your thoughts want to drive on.

It becomes your job to make your thoughts take the back roads, changing them to positive thoughts, and building up those pathways. This starts with recognizing your thoughts when they happen, and making them positive. Think of it this way. If you were to externalize your thoughts about how your body looks to your best friend, how would they respond? If you said that you were a complete failure because you messed up a project at work, they would not say, ,Yeah, you should probably just quit because you did a terrible job'. They would say, ,Okay, you may have screwed up that project but remember how successful you were on the last project, and the one before that? Let's find a way to fix it and make it better.' You are your own best friend. You are with yourself all the time. Give yourself the same compassion your best friend would.

Retrain your thinking by being more vigilant of your thoughts. Your subconscious thinking happens constantly, so it is your job to become more aware of the thoughts swirling around your head. To start, try to take a minute once every hour to address your internal thoughts. Have the majority of thought been positive or negative? Were the thoughts you were having rational? Often times the brain lets thoughts blow way out of proportion, and are often irrational. Get your subconscious in check by letting your rational brain decide whether those thoughts are worthy of your time.

For example, your thought may be, ,My boss is going to fire me because I failed the assignment. I won't be able to pay my mortgage, and I will get evicted. I'll have to live with my mother, and the kids will have to change school systems, and they will hate me.' Let your rational brain kick in here and bring you back to zero. You have not been fired, therefore you still can pay the bills. None of your worst fears are happening at this time, so calm down. Go back to the original problem, the failed assignment. Figure out a way to solve your problem head on. Talk to your boss. Find a way to revamp the project to turn it into a success. Avoiding the problem and waiting to get fired is not a good solution.

Say something good to yourself when you make small accomplishments. Give yourself an internal pat on the back when you have finished the dishes, folded and put away laundry, got through a difficult meeting, made it home on time. Remember that even the small, mundane things are worthy of celebration, because for some, just getting out of bed is a major success. Remember that you have it good, and anything you do during the day is cause for a pat on the back.

Begin saying daily affirmations to yourself every morning before your day starts. What you hear within the first hour of waking up sets the tone for the whole day, so make sure it is positive. Upon waking, sit up in bed, turn on the light and look around. You woke up today on the right side of the ground, so you have to be thankful. Also be thankful that you have a roof above your head and a bed to sleep in. You are ahead of the curve. As you begin your morning routine, take gratitude in all of the things you have. Recognize the breakfast you are eating as a gift, and as a measure of your past successes. Remember that the laundry, the sweeping and the dishes are proof that you have clothing, a house to live in and food to eat.

As you get dressed and ready, recognize that your body has carried you so far in life, and that it is a gift. It should not be criticized for being too big or having imperfections. Look at yourself in the mirror and set the tone for the day. Say, out loud, your daily affirmations:

I am strong, I am here, and I am successful. I have accomplished so much in my life, and today will be no different. I will start today with positivity. I will go through the day with energy and purpose.

I will end the day feeling accomplished, but not tired. I am good enough, and nobody can take my confidence from me. I am me, and there is no equal.

Your daily affirmation can be whatever you want it to be, but it should be motivating, it should be enlightening, and it should be true. It should not be about how great your hair looks, or how nice your clothes are. It should be about your strengths as a person, not physical appearance. That can change at any time, and putting all your stock in looks and things will cause you to fail later on.

CHAPTER 12
Positive Imagery

Fill your life with positive images to back up your positive thoughts. Whether you realize it or not, everything that you experience and look at through the day has an effect on you. If you surround yourself with unpaid bills and a cluttered home, your mood will be anxious and chaotic. If you fill your surroundings with family pictures and a clean home, you will feel much more uplifted and calm. While you may not be able to fill your entire world with positive pictures, you can work on your environment, and use internal pictures for when things are out of your control.

Start with your home. Everyone should have a nice place to come home to. Paint your walls a bright, calming color. Decorate with pictures of great days with the family, and objects that make you smile or remind you of a great experience. Vacation photos and souvenirs from family outings invoke feelings that bring the experience back. Surround yourself with things with meaning. A cluttered home usually means you have a cluttered mind. Avoid having too many knick-knacks and clutter all over your home that distract your mind. Have only what you need to feel comfortable. Make an effort to get the dishes done and the laundry folded so you don't come home to a mess.

Make your office an extension of your home, if you can. Bring in pictures that remind you of nice things, and put a stamp of your personality on your space. If you don't work somewhere that you have a specific office or personal space, make the best of a locker or drawer that may be yours. Even putting a picture of your loved ones on your phone or computer to look at occasionally is a step in the right direction.

If you find yourself in a situation where there is no beauty, no positivity and no hope, turn to your mind. Your brain has the capacity to take you back to a time and place where you felt calm and serene, giving you a moment to escape and detach from your situation. This practice can be immediately calming, and will help you get through a stressful event. Take a deep breath and close your eyes.

Imagine you are home, sitting on the couch with a good book. Think about how warm you feel under a blanket, and clutching a cup of your favorite tea. Go back to that thought and remember how calm you were, with no need to get up and rush out the door. You were simply content right there, enjoying the moment.

You could also use something more generic, like thinking about something you would like to do. For example, if you have booked a vacation for later this year, use it as a tool to motivate you and get you there. Imagine you are sitting in the sand, with the warm sun on your face, listening to the waves, and the seagulls. Whatever image you use, take a few opportune moments to really develop the thought. A fleeting, waves crashing on the beach image will not do much. Take the time to think about how the sand would feel between your toes to really put yourself in a more calm frame of mind.

CHAPTER 13

Aromatherapy

Have you ever smelled something that immediately brought back a great childhood memory? Maybe the smell of fried dough at the fair, or salt air from a family vacation at the beach? The power of smell has a strong connection to memory and feeling. Negative smells from certain foods or from garbage illicit a negative emotional response as well. As far as stress relief is concerned, aromatherapy uses certain smells to give specific responses in the brain, and remind you of good memories. Certain smells also produce a calming effect on the brain as well.

The presence of any smell with cause the brain to focus on it, minimizing other thoughts. Think about how the smell of food in a restaurant can distract you from a conversation, or if the kitchen garbage smells strong enough, you must give if your full attention and take it out before you do anything else. For stress relief, the introduction of good smells like lavender or mint give the brain something positive to focus on, while giving less attention to the stressors in your life. While this may only be a temporary solution, your body will have time to regulate your blood pressure and calm your tense muscles.

Aromatherapy is commonly used in tandem with massage therapy to increase the calming effect. The smell of essential oils calms the brain while the masseuse works to relieve tension in the muscles. Scent from essential oils is also great to use at home. An oil diffuser uses heat from flame to send oil particles into the air, filling the space with the aroma. Certain scents, like lavender or chamomile are great for stress relief, but any smell that you enjoy can be used to help calm you. Oils from mint or citrus can be very uplifting and energizing to your body and spirit.

While diffusers are great, essential oils can be used in other ways as well. Potpurri made of lavender can be placed in a bedroom to help you fall asleep, and air fresheners can be used in the car to calm you while driving. Essential oils like orange and lemon are often used in cleaning products to make the home feel fresh, although they are usually filled with chemicals as well. Homemade cleaners using essential oils, vinegar and natural castile soap are a great natural alternative that you won't feel guilty about inhaling.

Add a few drops to your hot bath water to disperse scent in the air. Essential oils can also be used in place of dryer sheets that often have a very strong smell. Add a few drops on a damp washcloth and throw it in with a load of clothes. The scent will dry into the clothes, giving you fresh, calming scents all day long.

Use smell wherever you go for a relaxing boost of energy. You could even keep a bottle of your favorite oil in your bag or desk drawer to open and smell when you need a pick me up. Just be careful that it is well sealed. If the concentrated oil spills, it can ruin fabric and create an overwhelming scent in the air.

Essential oils have been used since ancient times for all sorts of ailments, including stomach ache, indigestion, headache and many other things. The power of smell has the ability to cure the body and mind. They can be used only to smell, as part of a topical product like lotion, or taken orally. Be careful and do your research before using, because if taken wrong, especially orally, the concentrated doses can make you sick. It is important to consult with your health care provider before taking anything orally.

CONCLUSION

Thank you for making it through to the end of this book, let's hope it was informative and able to provide you with all of the tools you need to achieve your goals whatever they may be.

The next step is to start trying some of these techniques in your life, and find out what works best for you.

Finally, if you found this book useful in anyway, a review on Amazon is always appreciated!

www.ingramcontent.com/pod-product-compliance
Lightning Source LLC
Chambersburg PA
CBHW071508070526
44578CB00001B/481